The DIY Wedding: How to Bootstrap Your Way to the Perfect Wedding

Jennifer Cox

Table of Contents

Chapter 1: What to Consider Before Planning Your Bootstrap Wedding

Have you ever been to a wedding and marveled at a creative idea they had when putting together the party favors or the décor? Beautiful moving moments are free and you and your partner deserve as many of those as you can pack into your special day. Your wedding should be the best day of your life regardless of what size budget you have.

Some of the most successful weddings have been planned on a bootstrap budget. There is nothing that says you can't have the same thing. In fact, you can have the wedding and honeymoon of your dreams if you plan it right.

Before we begin, it is important to get into the right mindset. The wedding picture you have in your head may not be the wedding you have the budget for, so it is time to get creative. You have to be willing to have an open mind to creative alternatives that are still gorgeous but are within your budget.

The following tips and suggestions will help you discover ideas on how to plan a wedding that is both practical, yet the social event that you and your spouse will remember for years. Your friends and family will have a great time. You will not have to stress about a giant bill that comes at the end of your special day and you both can ride off into the sunset knowing that you created something beautiful and

financially responsible to set the tone for the rest of
your lives together.

Chapter 2: So Where Should You Get Hitched?

Here's the good news about venues. There are a multitude of opportunities to get creative when selecting one and many do not cost a lot. Take a look at these tips for saving money on wedding venues.

Get married on a Friday or a Sunday. Why? Because it is typically less expensive than a wedding on Saturday. It is still during the weekend when guests can attend. Friday is the start of the week, so you can start your honeymoon with the entire weekend ahead of you in case you are choosing a short weekend holiday. If you choose Sunday, you are starting the week fresh with your honeymoon.

A bootstrap DIY wedding means that you are going to have to make some hard choices. You may not be able to have everything you envisioned in your head. Take some time to decide what you want most and spend your money on that one thing. As a result, you will save money by cutting corners on the smaller things. If you find that you cannot bring yourself to cut out a particular thing, the perhaps it means more to you than you realize. Evaluate why you can't let go of it and see if you can either include it in your budget or find alternatives.

Consider alternative venues. Why would you want the same kind of wedding that everyone else has? A benefit of having a tight budget is that it forces you to get creative. In fact, one wedding trend is to combine glamour with down home flair. Spend a lot on your dream wedding dress and then hold your reception on the beach or in the back yard. The more informal the better. Not only does it alleviate serious anxiety worrying about everything turning out perfectly, it puts your guests at ease. They know they are going to have a good time in comfortable surroundings. Don't have a decent size back yard? Check in to other possibilities like a great national park that is rich in natural beauty.

Consider searching for venues on the outskirts of a big city or in a small town. The fees for securing a venue can be considerably less. Even better, if you can find an abandoned barn or building that has a vintage charm, that would be perfect for mixing old world ambience with modern day elegance.

Combine your wedding ceremony and reception into one location. Not only is it less expensive than renting two locations, but guests will love the fact that they only have to travel to one destination.

What time? This may not have crossed your mind, but the time of day to have a wedding can have a significant impact on your budget. Morning weddings are typically less expensive than afternoon or evening events because it is cost effective to serve breakfast or brunch than it is to serve dinner. Also, the earlier the ceremony, the more time you have to spend with your spouse on your wedding day. Take this into consideration and see if this would be an option for you.

Along with the time of day, the time of the year matters when considering booking a budget-friendly venue. Summer is considered the wedding season which means that most everything will be more expensive. Consider having your wedding at a different time of year. Not only will you stand out on your friends and family's calendar, but you can save a lot of money doing it.

This is very important. Make sure that when you are researching venues, you do not mention the event is a wedding until after you get a quote on the price. There are many places that will raise their prices once they realize you intend to use their space for a wedding. It may not be fair, but it is a fact.

Some places will give you a discount when you offer to make a full payment instead of just putting down a deposit. See if the places you are looking at are willing to do this, but make sure you have a reimbursement clause in the contract to protect yourself in case an unexpected change in plan occurs.

In your mind, do you have everyone you've ever met attending your wedding? That may be difficult to realize on a bootstrap budget. Let me suggest that you consider keeping the event small and intimate. Perhaps inviting 50 people or less and limiting it to close friends and family.

A wonderful alternative to a big reception is to throw a big informal party when you return from your honeymoon. It's a great way to share your experiences with them while celebrating with as many people as you like.

There is a wonderful, stress-free option when planning your wedding. It is usually referred to as all-inclusive wedding packages. This is great because it covers everything— the venue, the food, the music, the flowers— everything! All you have to do is select the package you want and they do the rest. This option is so fantastic because it allows you to choose from venues that may not otherwise be in your budget. Make sure you do your homework however, and read the fine print to ensure that what you want is covered in the package.

There is nothing that says your wedding reception has to go into the early morning hours. Shortening the reception can not only save you money, but it allows you and your new spouse to get an early start on the honeymoon. If a reception is too long, what you see are many guests winding down and sitting around while you are paying for staff to also wait around until time to clean up. It may be best to put some of those savings toward your honeymoon or on some other part of the wedding.

Another factor to consider is to make sure that you are only renting space that you need and not more. If the venue has two spaces that connect to each other making the place look spacious may be great, but it is going to be more expensive. Consider whether you really need that extra space. Look at your confirmed R.S.V.P.s and decide how much space you really need and then book that.

Bring your own alcohol to the venue instead of hiring someone else to do it. This can save you a lot on your budget, just make sure that your venue allows it.

Chapter 3: How Should We Invite Them?

Today's perception of weddings are more contemporary than they have ever been. The rules have loosened up a bit about proper etiquette. That means there is a lot of room to try new things, be a bit more informal and shake it up a bit. Here are a few suggestions that can save you money on your invitations.

Your save the date cards should only be sent to your closest friends and family members. All your other guests can receive just the invitation, or you can skip the save the date cards and only send out invitations. That saves on stamps and other costs.

Another option is to send save the date postcards instead. This costs less in stamp expenses than regular cards and are inexpensive to make or buy. You can print out a photo of the two of you on one side and on the other side have a postcard format.

If you want to cut costs down even more, then hand deliver your save the date cards and invitations to local friends and family. They will appreciate that you took the time to deliver them yourself.

The wedding industry is very competitive these days, so take advantage of that. Businesses to will gladly offer you the best price in order to get your business and prevent you from going to their competition. Look online for custom invitations. There are several to choose from that offer detailed and individualized invitations for less money.

The least expensive option may be to do it yourself. All you need is quality paper stock and a printer. You can even make your own envelopes with a template or by using a cricket machine. If that's too much work, purchase blank printable invitations that you can simply run through your printer.

A free option would be to create email invites or "evites." Send an email to everyone on your list and then later confirm that they received it. This is a great option when you have little money to devote to this area of your wedding.

Chapter 4: What Are We Going To Wear?

When you are thinking about choosing an inexpensive wedding dress option, usually what comes to mind is to make your own or have someone make it for you. That may or may not be less expensive. Fabric is expensive these days and the cost of hiring someone to make it for you could exceed your budget compared to buying one off the rack. However, if you are seriously considering it, then there are a few things you need to take into account.

First, making a wedding dress takes time, so you need to make sure you plan ahead to hire a seamstress and that they will have enough time to design and make the dress.

Do your research and make sure that you are cutting costs by making your own dress. Keep in mind that your time is valuable and with so many other things going on with planning the wedding, it may be worth it to you, to buy your dress.

Make sure you have a clear design in mind of the kind of dress you want. This can take a significant amount of time. Consider your body type and what styles look best on you. Do not rely on a picture in a magazine to make this decision.

Don't forget that there are other options than just making your own dress or buying one. You can rent a dress as well. After the wedding, many brides do not want to carve out a lot of room to store a wedding dress they will never wear again.

The groom's suit, as well as the rest of the wedding party's clothing, can also be rented. Or you can buy a regular dress off the department store rack and embellish it to make it your own. If you do this, some things to keep in mind are the color and pattern of the dress. Will it fit in with your theme? Most importantly, is it comfortable? You will be wearing it through the entire ceremony and reception. One of the benefits of doing this is that you could wear it again if you wanted the option.

Chapter 5: The Bling is in the Ring

The status symbol bling ring isn't important to everyone these days as it might have been in the past, especially when budget is a consideration. However, there are ways to have a beautiful wedding band set without spending a lot of money.

A quirky, but extremely effective method is to either make your own or have someone make it for you using a quarter. There are several tutorials online that show you how to do it. If you know someone who knows how to do it, you could ask them to make it for you. Maybe they would do it for you as a wedding gift and all it would cost you would be the value of the coins. Having something handmade like this is always a sentimental treasure.

If you don't want to go through the trouble of making your own wedding bands, there are certainly other options. You can buy cubic zirconia, which looks just like real diamonds without the cost. This is great because knowing how much a real diamond costs, you don't have to worry about losing it, or freaking out if it gets lost. Yes, if you lost it the sentimental value would be disappointing, but you would at least know that you're not out a bunch of money in order to replace it.

A neutral band that isn't necessarily a wedding band, but could represent one is another option. For example, if you went on a vacation and strolled through one of the souvenir shops and found matching bands that you both loved, you could use that instead of paying more money for a traditional wedding band set.

For those quirky adventurous souls, you can always consider getting a tattoo on your ring finger in place of a ring. This is a good idea for a lot of men who work with their hands and who are constantly having to take their wedding band off during the day. You could choose your designs together and get matching tattoos, or have your initials on each other's ring fingers. Yes, it is an alternative idea, but it works for some.

Chapter 6: Food to Feed the Wedding Soul

Food can be one of the higher-priced items in your wedding budget. The cost of hiring a caterer and someone to coordinate the event, not to mention hiring workers to serve at the wedding reception, can be costly. Your wedding can still be beautiful and memorable and budget friendly by considering some of these less expensive ideas.

Let's start with the wedding cake. These custom cakes can go as high as $1200 and more, depending on the design and size. Often, couples order a bigger cake than what they need, and with the labor costs of decorating it, it can really add up fast.

Instead of ordering a traditional wedding cake, you can order what is called a "dummy cake." The dummy cake is a Styrofoam base covered in fondant or icing and decorated just like a regular cake.

Unlike a regular traditional wedding cake, however, this saves the baker a tremendous amount of time thereby cutting down on labor costs. Then, you would have the baker make sheet cakes, where they would slice it up in the kitchen and serve it on plates ready for your wedding guests.

This is an amazing option to save a lot of money on your wedding food budget. If you are concerned with the cake cutting part of the reception, then have the baker make the top tier a real cake and that way you can cut into it, eat it and save the rest for your one year anniversary.

Cupcakes are another option. They are small, individualized servings and guests can easily pick them up.

Cupcakes can also be designed to aid in the overall decor of the reception. For example, each cupcake can be made to look like a flower, or bunching all the cupcakes together can make an overall design that can include writing or other embellishments, just like on a regular cake. Then guests just take cupcakes away from that. This idea saves a lot of leftover unwanted cake.

Catering your own wedding. Keep in mind this is going to take up a lot of your time so be sure to plan accordingly. One good idea is to have a desert bar with several different types of candies and cookies that are easy for your guests to pick up. If you want to kill two birds with one stone, put some coordinated paper gift bags on the table and guests can fill their bags with the items from the dessert bar and take it home as a party favor bag of goodies.

You will either be spending time or money on your wedding, so if you do not have enough money in your budget, then plan ahead to use some of your time to create your own catered affair.

Chapter 7: Creating the Ambience of Your Big Day

Wedding decor is one of those categories that can be the easiest to save money on if you are creative. If you are not creative, grab one of your friends or family members who is creative and get with them about planning a budget-friendly wedding and reception.

There are many areas when decorating your event that you can cut corners on and still have a beautiful display. For example, you can make your own wedding backdrop with very little money and just a little elbow grease. If you want an arbor, you can use materials that you find at the hardware store like wood or PVC pipe and decorate or paint it.

Ribbon and fabric are also great tools you can use to dress up your wedding ceremony and reception areas. Get on YouTube or Pinterest and look for ribbon tutorials to see what you can do with it.

If you want a little more bling to your to decor, then add clear crystals that you can find in the shape of beaded curtains that dazzle different areas of your reception. You can hang them from an arch or on trees if it's an outdoor wedding, or from light fixtures if the reception is indoors.

Don not overlook natural greenery and foliage. They can also add a natural beauty, especially to an outdoor wedding. You can either find real greenery or purchase fake greenery at a craft store.

String lights are another option that can be hung from the ceiling, or even a point on the wall to make a good backdrop. Highlight certain areas that might be darker around the reception area to improve the lighting. Better lighting makes for better pictures, also.

Use your flowers to create a pretty backdrop where guests can take pictures and you and your spouse can take wedding pictures. They do not have to be real flowers. You can make paper flowers and they are just as beautiful as the real thing. Just be sure to give yourself enough time to make these in advance.

Color coordinated paper crafts are another option for wedding décor. Rosettes of varying sizes can create a wall display. You can also make paper pom-poms to hang from the ceiling to fill in more space. Creativity is key, so the more creative and open-minded you are to trying an idea, the more ideas you're going to have.

Do not forget to enlist your friends and family in helping you if you have decorations that you are going to make. They will enjoy being able to help and spending the time with you, creating something special for your big day.

Chapter 8: How to Have Fun at Your Own Wedding

When thinking about entertainment ideas, this is another area where you can get creative. Spending time with your friends and family is going to be a great day in itself, but there are things that you can plan that will enhance everyone's experience.

Depending on your budget, consider one or more of the following:

Inflatable slides and bounce houses are a great distraction for the younger kids and younger adults. This is a wonderful way to get them laughing and celebrating. Giant games like wedding twister or corn hole games can be a lot of fun too. Horseshoes or ring toss is another option.

If one of your friends can draw caricatures, enlist their help. A personalized drawing is wonderful party favor that your guests can take home. If you don't know anyone who can draw, you can check into seeing how much it would cost to hire somebody for the evening.

Food trucks are a big hit with many weddings. It might sound weird, but guests love a Taco Bell truck or an ice cream truck where they can walk right up and choose what they want.

You can have game cards at each table that require filling out your predictions on how many children the bride and groom will have. Guests who aren't dancing can sit there and engage with other guests playing these games. They are great conversation starters and keep guests entertained.

A DIY photo booth is a huge party pleaser. Just make several props ahead of time that they can use to put on and then take photographs using either a photographer or their own cameras and smartphones. This is also a wonderful way to cut down on photography costs and get a record of all the wedding that guests that were there on your special day.

The wedding piñata can be a great feature for both the bride and groom and the wedding guests as a feature of the reception. Create a kid zone area where children can be entertained and have fun with age-appropriate games.

If you worry about spending money on a DJ or a band, then maybe you want to take some time and put together a compilation CD of all your favorite songs and play that at the wedding instead. You could grab a friend or family member to be in charge of running the music and not have to worry about inappropriate songs because you've already screened them.

Karaoke is another fun idea where guests can take turns singing their favorite songs. Of course all of this has to be videotaped, so the bride and groom can watch it back.

Put a friend in charge of making a love story video that recounts the time you and your spouse met up until present day. This is a nice tribute to your relationship and your new marriage.

Make a list of your friends and what their professions are and then asked them if they can donate their time or service as a wedding gift.

Chapter 9: Riding off into the Sunset

There are more adventurous ways to ride in style and make an entrance than ever before. No longer are limousines the standard transportation vehicle for weddings. Contemporary weddings celebrate different themes and think outside of the box, so it is no surprise when couples planning their events decide to consider alternative transportation methods. Here are just a few ideas on how to ride out into the sunset with your new spouse.

Bicycles. Before you shrug off this idea. Allow me the chance to convince you. Bicycles are simplistic and charming way to put some classy humor into your wedding send off. If you are going a short distance, it doesn't make sense to rent a vehicle. Instead, use a cute tandem bike built for two, or a pair of bicycles that you and your spouse can capture great photographs on before riding off.

Pedicab. A cross between a bicycle and a carriage, this idea is great for when you are holding your wedding reception or wedding ceremony at a very small downtown area with cozy quiet side streets and you need to travel a short distance to reach your destination. They are also quite a bit less expensive than a horse-drawn carriage.

Boat and canoes. If your wedding venue is near a lake or beach, a great idea is to utilize the water is a way to get from one place to another. A quaint little canoe for two would be just the romantic notion to greet your guests as you paddle up to them on the bank to get to your wedding reception. A sailboat cruise can be another option if your reception is held near a harbor or Marina.

The truck. Riding in the back of a pickup truck can be just the finishing touch that your quaint country wedding needs to keep with the down-home style and tone. Surely somebody you know has one you can borrow, or you can rent one for the day.

Golf cart. For the golf enthusiasts, or for getting around the venue that has wide open green landscaping, a golf cart may be the ideal mode of transportation. You can decorate these and cute way that matches the theme of your wedding. Have one of your friends or family members show for you from the wedding ceremony to the reception.

Motorcycles. Looking to live a bit on the wild side? Motorcycles can help add to that theme. They are great for getting what you need to go in quickly and also act as an awesome prop for those wedding pictures. They may not fit every wedding theme, but those themes they do fit really rock.

Horseback. This is one of the more romantic ideas with the notion that you would literally be riding off into the sunset with your teammate. Either put the bride on the horse and have the groom walk beside her, or both of you mount the horse and ride off together.

Walk. If all else fails and it is a short distance, then stroll hand-in-hand to your destination.

Antique cars.   This mode of transportation is a classic way to bring the old and modern together.   Do you know of any friends or relatives that have a vintage vehicle that you can borrow for the wedding? Ask them to see if they will lend their vehicle to you. And hey, maybe they would even be willing to chauffer for you.

Chapter 10: Happily Ever After Honeymoon

No doubt when you think about weddings, you are going to think about the honeymoon. What type of honeymoon should you take and how can you make it bootstrap affordable? It depends on what you both like. What common interests do you have? Have you talked about where you would like to go on your honeymoon and do you both agree? Here are a list of options that are budget-friendly honeymoon destinations.

Camping. There is nothing like spending several days in close quarters without running water, and in many cases a toilet to see how you are going to get along. Camping can be as fun and as adventurous as you want it to be. Just make sure that you actually like camping before you make it your honeymoon destination. It is true that you can save a lot of money by going camping, but only as long as you know what you are doing, lest you get stuck in an unexpected emergency. It is supposed to be fun, so make sure you prepare ahead of time.

Road trip. Taking off toward an unknown destination can be an exciting adventure in itself. Throw in a destination that you've always wanted to go to and you have the makings of a perfect honeymoon. It is important that you preplan and budget for things like gas, food and lodging, but there are many deals online to help you with that. If you do your research, you can make it easy on your wallet.

Cruising.   Cruises aren't as expensive as they used to be.   Nowadays you can buy tickets for a relatively low amount of money depending on your location destination and the time of year.   You could take a quick trip to the Bahamas or a two week round trip to Alaska.   It is up to you.   While on board, all food is included in your ticket price. You have the choice to stay on the boat or get off at each port.   Just make sure that you get on the boat in time before it pushes off to the next destination.

All-inclusive honeymoon destination.   There are resorts that specifically cater to newlywed couples, offering an all-inclusive honeymoon package.   You pay one fee and all the food, entertainment and lodging is included.   Do your research and you can find some pretty great deals in the off-season.

Festivals.   If you time your wedding right you can take advantage of a local fair or festival that is coming up in your city or town.   In fact, this could be a really cool idea as a wedding reception idea where guests can get in and enjoy all the festivities together. Contact the manager of the events and see if you can arrange some kind of special area for your wedding party.   If you are just interested in this idea as a honeymoon destination for the both of you, this would be a great place to have a lot of fun together.

Stay home.   At first glance this may not seem like a honeymoon vacation at all.   However, you can find a lot of magical moments right where you live if you are looking for them.   Take a walk downtown.   Discover your historic sightseeing points of interests and learn something new you didn't know about your city.   Do these things together and it will feel like a honeymoon. Rent a hotel in your city, and it will feel like you are away from home in a different destination.

Use a few or all of these ideas and tips to create your perfect DIY bootstrap wedding. May you have all the luck and good fortune in your upcoming marriage.